WASHI
TAPE
CHRISTMAS

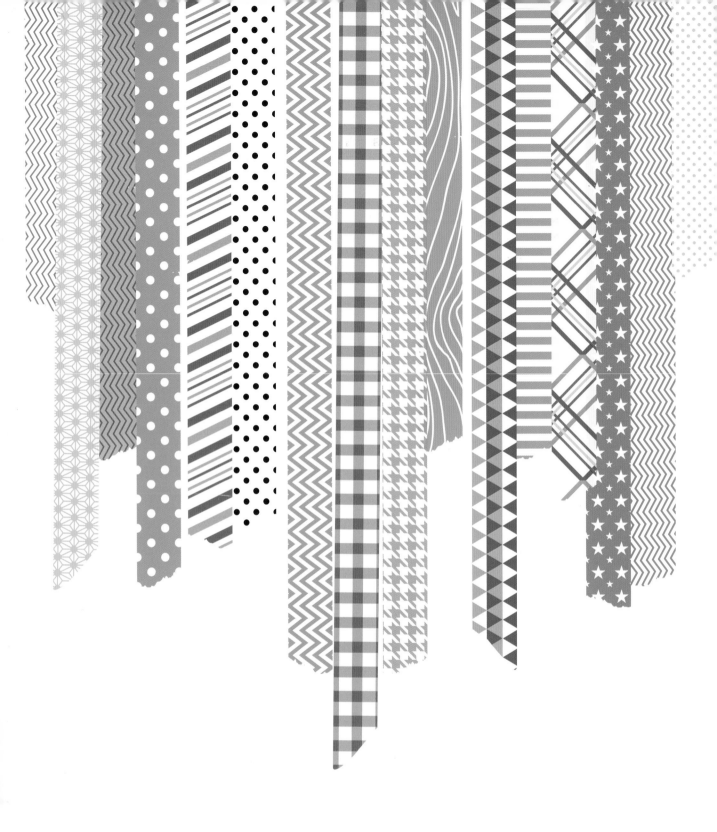

WASHI TAPE CHRISTMAS

EASY HOLIDAY CRAFT IDEAS WITH WASHI TAPE

KAMI BIGLER

David and Charles

www.stitchcraftcreate.co.uk

C⭑NTENTS

INTRODUCTION

When it comes to crafting, there's no better place to start than the holiday season. Whether you make something beautiful to decorate your home or to give away as a gift, there will always be something special about these handmade details that you just can't buy from a store.

If you're just getting started with washi tape, this decorative masking tape originally from Japan is one of the best ways to add a little personality to any project. Keep a roll in your purse to create a last minute note to a friend, and keep jars of it at home to provide the materials for a fun-filled 'crafternoon' with friends.

One of the best things about washi tape, besides the countless darling patterns and designs that it comes in, is the way it tears so easily with your hands; the classic torn edge look is what makes it truly stand apart from a plastic tape.

The goal of this book is to inspire you to become creative with washi tape, and to try using it in new ways while you celebrate the Christmas season.

MATERIALS AND EQUIPMENT

While washi tape is the star of this book, there's a bunch of other key players that will make your craft projects come to life. I'm a fan of keeping things simple whenever possible, but you might need to take a trip to the craft store to buy a few items to get started.

Here's the ultimate list of materials and equipment needed to create the craft projects featured in this book:

- kraft paper card set (card bases with envelopes)
- white card stock
- paper slicer (guillotine)
- white butcher paper (kraft paper)
- circle craft punch
- die cutting tool, such as the CuttleBug by Cricut
- circle cutting dies
- fine-tip scissors
- pinking shears
- scoring board, such as the mini scoring board from Martha Stewart Crafts
- baker's twine
- ordinary twine or string
- glue dots

- low temperature hot glue gun
- star stickers
- snowflake embellishments
- styrofoam wreath form
- natural clothes pins (pegs)
- natural wood frame
- wooden spools
- tiny bottlebrushes
- papier-mâché cones
- round plastic beads
- tea light candles
- clear plastic tubes
- cupcake liners

It's best to shop per project as you create, and you may come across a few other items you need as you go. This is an overview so you can get an idea of what you already have at home and what you need to pick up before getting started.

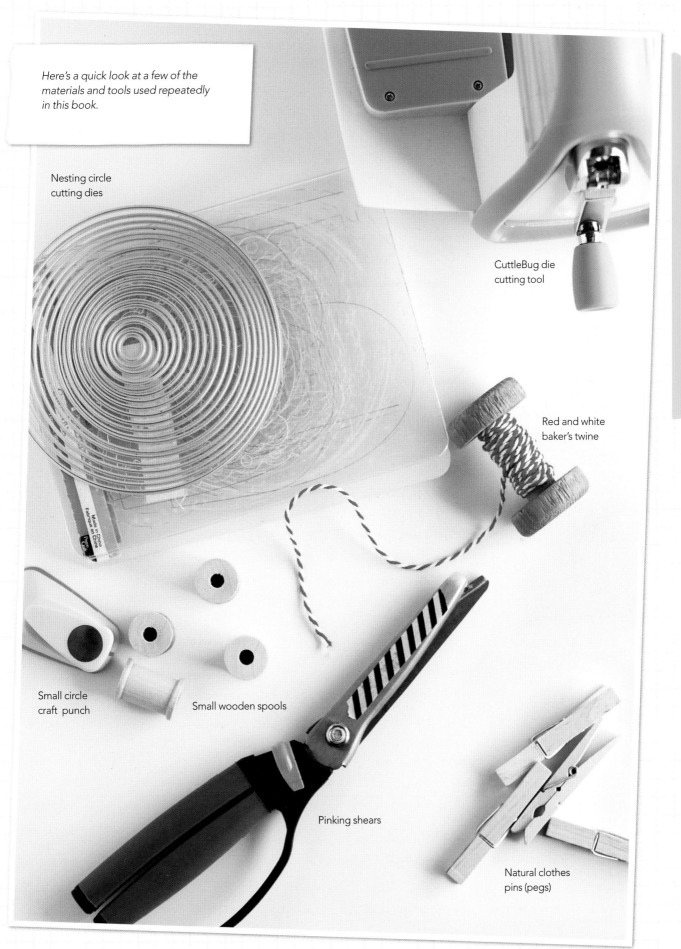

Here's a quick look at a few of the materials and tools used repeatedly in this book.

Nesting circle cutting dies

CuttleBug die cutting tool

Red and white baker's twine

Small circle craft punch

Small wooden spools

Pinking shears

Natural clothes pins (pegs)

CLEVER CARDS

One of the biggest highlights of the Christmas season is going out to the mailbox with the hopes of finding something happy in it; 'happy mail' as we like to call it. Whether you choose to send out photo cards or handmade cards with an added photo inside, you're bound to make someone happy when they open their mailbox and find these inside. All the following festive card projects are simple to make, and if you make one you might as well make a few!

WINTER WONDERLAND

Celebrate the beauty of winter with this pretty snowflake card. An array of blue tones along with shiny snowflakes makes this card sparkle and shine. Your ever-growing collection of washi tape will be put to good use.

You will need:

- blue and white washi tape in assorted designs
- 12.5 x 18cm (5 x 7in) kraft paper card base with envelope
- scissors, or craft knife (optional)
- mini glue dots
- snowflake stickers, confetti, or decals
- tiny gemstone embellishments
- bone folder

1 Run the bone folder over the crease of the card to ensure the fold is clean and that the card will lie flat when folded.

2 In a random order, cut or tear strips of washi tape then layer rows in different designs across the front of the card. You can repeat the pattern as you work up the card, or keep it random.

3 I like the torn edge washi tape look, but this will be covered by the snowflake embellishments on the front of the card. To retain some torn edges, you can wrap small sections of washi tape with torn

edges around the fold to the back of the card, or you can cut the washi tape in a straight edge at the fold using scissors or a craft knife.

4 Using the mini glue dots, stick a snowflake embellishment at the end of each line of washi tape on the front of the card. Then make these snowflakes sparkle by sticking tiny gemstones to their centers with mini glue dots.

Now you have a darling card or party invite that will celebrate the frozen season ahead.

HAPPY HOLIDAY BERRIES

By layering different patterns of green washi tape you can create a festive holly berry wreath and finish it off with a little red berry detail. Then peek through it to catch a glimpse of the inside of the card. I love adding pink to classic Christmas colors, but feel free to add in any color of card stock you like to your own project.

You will need:

- green washi tapes in assorted designs
- 12.5 x 18cm (5 x 7in) kraft paper card base with envelope
- 10 x 15cm (4 x 6in) pink card stock mount
- small red card stock confetti circles, buttons, or dots
- fine-tip scissors
- die cutting tool, such as the CuttleBug from Cricut
- circle cutting dies in your choice of size
- glue dots
- three-dimensional foam adhesive square
- lace washi tape (optional, for the inside of the card)

1 Place glue dots in each corner of the pink card stock mount then adhere it to the kraft paper card base. Open the card out flat then run it through your die cutting tool to cut out a circle on the front. The cutting die can cut through both the kraft card base and the pink card stock, but if you prefer you can run these through separately.

2 Pull out a length of green washi tape measuring 10cm (4in) and tape it directly back on itself, so that the sticky sides are together. Now fold the segment in half and use your fine-tip scissors to notch out the letter V at the ends to create a more fancy finished look (A).

3 Add a glue dot between the washi halves then adhere them together off-center, so that you can see both the top and bottom layer. Grab a second glue dot and adhere the washi tape to the edge of the circle.

4 Repeat steps 2 and 3 with all the different green washi tapes to work your way around the central circle of the card (B). I used about 14 different washi tape segments to fill the wreath on my card.

5 To finish the wreath, add little red paper circles in a cluster like you'd see on a holly berry wreath.

If you like, you can tape the inside of the card with a pretty tape, lining up the pattern. I used a lace tape and I love how it looks, just peeking through. That's it!

To make the card a little more three-dimensional, lift the top layers of washi tape off the card a bit.

A

B

CRISSCROSS CHRISTMAS TREE

This simple card design really shows off the classic torn edge effect you can get using washi tape, which I love. When you layer a variety of different tapes together you can create the look of a pretty tree, the classic symbol of Christmas.

1 To begin, adhere the white card stock mount to the kraft paper card base.

2 Starting at the base, begin layering diagonal strips of washi tape on top of each other to create your tree. Gradually introduce smaller strips of tape as you get closer to the top.

3 Use the star craft punch to punch out a small star from the gold glitter card stock then stick it to the top of the tree using a three-dimensional foam adhesive square.

4 To finish, add small gold stars at a few of the torn edges to look like small ornaments hanging from the tree.

Feel free to handwrite or stamp a favorite holiday greeting right on the front or inside of your card for a nice finishing touch.

ALL STACKED UP

Tis' the season for giving gifts, and sometimes the card itself can be the gift, so this card is perfect for those occasions. Whether you fill it with money or a gift token, or just a heartfelt note to someone special, this simple card is perfect to create using your washi tape collection. The baker's twine bow makes it look like a stack of gifts all wrapped up.

You will need:

- washi tape in assorted festive designs
- 12.5 x 18cm (5 x 7in) kraft paper card base with envelope
- 10 x 15cm (4 x 6in) white card stock mount
- red and white striped baker's twine
- glue dots

1 Start by adding glue dots to each corner of the white card stock mount and center then adhere it to the kraft paper card base.

2 In neat horizontal rows, start layering different pieces of your festive washi tapes one above the next. I used six pieces, but you can add more or less depending on the width of tapes you use.

3 Finish off the card by taping on two pieces of baker's twine. Stick one segment under the bottom piece of tape and run it straight up the stack, using a glue dot to adhere it to the top of the gift. Then tie the second segment of baker's twine into a tight little bow and press this into the same glue dot at the top.

This sweet handmade card is bound to put a smile on someone's face.

STAR OF WONDER, STAR OF LIGHT

If you love all things that sparkle and shine, then this card is for you. There's so much symbolism surrounding stars for Christmas, and this card is a great way to celebrate and remember the real meaning of the season. The big gold glittery heart in the center is neat, in that it's seen from both the outside and inside of the card. Add a favorite sentiment for someone special to really personalize it.

You will need:

- gold washi tape
- washi tape in a tiny star design
- clear washi tape in a lace design
- 12.5 x 18cm (5 x 7in) kraft paper card base with envelope
- gold glitter card stock
- white card stock
- small star craft punch
- die cutting tool, such as the CuttleBug from Cricut
- 1cm (1½in) star cutting die
- 5cm (2in) circle cutting die
- tiny glue dots
- three-dimensional foam adhesive square

1 Open the card out flat and run it through your die cutting tool to cut out a circle on the front. Then use the die cutting tool and the star cutting die to cut out a star from the gold glitter card stock.

2 Cover the inside of the card with lace washi tape, taking care to line up the pattern of the joined pieces to create an impression of one solid piece (A). Using the three-dimensional adhesive square, add the gold glitter star to sit in the center of the circle when the card is closed.

3 Now tape a length of the solid gold and a length of patterned star washi tape, both measuring 10cm (4in), onto the piece of white card stock. Using your small star craft punch, punch out tiny stars to create a pile of both patterns.

4 Stick your small stars around the cut out circle on the front of the card using tiny glue dots (B). You can create any pattern around the circle you'd like.

That's it! Now you have a pretty sparkly card to give someone special.

Although I used lace washi tape design for the background, any sort of pretty white washi tape patterns will work here.

DARLING
DECORATIONS

Home decor will be one of the most fun ways to put your washi tape collection to good use, because you'll be able to enjoy your creations all season long, year after year. Whether you keep them for yourself or give them as gifts, you'll treasure these darling decorations more than the rest because they're handmade. And when your neighbors and friends stop by and ask where you bought your beautiful creations, you can proudly tell them that they're handmade, by you!

You will need:

- red and green washi tape in assorted designs
- 3 pieces of 22 x 28cm (8½ x 11in) white printer paper
- stapler
- pinking shears (optional)

LET THE COUNTDOWN BEGIN!

Counting down the days until Christmas is one of the best things about being a kid. So to help build up anticipation for the big day (not that help is needed, wink!), include your kids in making this simple Christmas countdown chain. Turn up your favorite Christmas music, turn on the lights of your tree, and enjoy a fun 'crafternoon' with your little ones making this Christmas countdown chain together.

1 Working with one piece of white printer paper at a time, start by adding long strips of red washi tape designs to your first piece. Leave white spaces between each strip of tape you apply, and completely fill one side of your paper with rows of different red tape designs.

2 Flip the same piece of paper over. Taping the washi tape in the same direction, add a variety of green washi tape designs in strips across the paper, again leaving white spaces between each strip you apply.

3 Now cut rows of the taped paper in the opposite direction to the rows of tape you applied with regular scissors, or with pinking shears if you'd like to create create a cute edge, as shown.

4 To make the chain, simply use a stapler to join the loops of paper together. You can create a pattern with your colors by keeping all the reds on the outside and the greens on the inside of each loop; once they're stapled all together, you'll love the way they look like this.

Hang the chain up on your wall or mantle and remove a link every day as you countdown to Christmas.

PATCHWORK CHRISTMAS WREATH

You will need:

- green washi tape in assorted designs
- holly berry template (see Templates)
- red card stock circles
- sharp fine-tip scissors
- green velvet ribbon
- red ribbon for a bow, or a red pre-made bow
- glue dots
- styrofoam wreath form
- push pins

This wreath would look great hanging over your mantle or attached to your front door. The variety of different washi tapes used for this decoration bring it that sweet handmade look, which you just can't find in a store.

1 Prepare your styrofoam wreath by wrapping it with green ribbon, ensuring that you secure the ribbon in position well with push pins.

2 Make 2½ photocopies of the holly berry template, then begin adding strips of different washi tape designs side by side to completely cover the holly leaves on the template (A). Once they are all covered, use your sharp scissors to carefully cut out each leaf outline.

3 Prepare to pin your items to the wreath by dividing your holly leaves and tiny red card stock circles into groups of three, along with push pins and glue dots for each grouping. This will make the crafting go much more quickly once you start.

4 Touch the end of a push pin into a glue dot to make the end of the pin sticky. Now touch that sticky pin end into one of the red circle rounds (B) then push it through the first holly leaf. Gather your leaves and berries up in groups of three then pin them to your wreath to make them look like real holly berry leaf clusters. Continue to work your way around the wreath in this manner until complete.

Finish your wreath by attaching a big red bow to the top, and enjoy!

I used red card circle embellishments from Candi by Craftwork, but you could also use tiny red buttons or red confetti rounds.

A

B

You will need:

- green washi tape in assorted designs
- holly berry template (see Templates)
- tiny red paper circles, tiny red buttons, or anything berrylike
- white card stock
- solid colored card stock
- fine-tip scissors
- glue dots
- three-dimensional foam adhesive squares
- natural clothes pins (pegs)
- simple stamp set

SAY MY NAME, SAY MY NAME

Whether your Christmas stockings are bought in a store or made at home, you can still add your child's name to them for that personal touch. Using the same technique we used for the Christmas wreath (see Patchwork Christmas Wreath), you can add holly berry leaf clusters to a natural clothes pin (peg) as a sweet way to clip a simple name tag to the top of each stocking.

1 Make a photocopy of the holly berry template then add rows of different green washi tape designs over it. Using your small fine-tip scissors, cut out each holly leaf.

2 To make one name holder, take a group of three leaves and use a glue dot to adhere them to the end of a clothes pin (peg). You could alternatively use your low temperature hot glue gun for this step.

3 Use a three-dimensional foam adhesive square to add a cluster of tiny red paper circles as berries at the base of leaves.

4 Now for the name tag. You can either stamp or print out the names onto your white card stock; we stamped our names using a stamp set, but if you have a favorite font you could easily print them instead.

5 Layer your printed piece of white card stock in front of a piece of solid colored card stock, both cut into pennant flag shapes. Use a glue dot to attach them together, staggering one in front of the other. Finish off your name tag with a simple underline in a favorite washi tape strip, which will look good with the holly berry clothes pin holders.

That's it, a fun way to label each stocking waiting for the big night.

FESTIVE FIRS

Create a festive garland to decorate a dessert table, a mantle, or even a headboard in your child's bedroom as a darling way to prepare for Christmas. We've made this decoration easy for you to create by providing a template you can copy on your home printer or photocopier.

You will need:

- green washi tape in assorted designs
- Christmas tree template (see Templates)
- small paper punch
- fine-tip scissors
- thin twine or string

1 Photocopy your Christmas tree template then begin adding strips of tape right onto it. You can add rows of the same pattern or you can mix things up and make your own pattern by alternating different tape designs.

2 Once the trees on your template are covered in washi tape, cut them all out. A pair of sharp fine-tip scissors will make the job easy.

3 Use your small paper punch to create a tiny hole at the top of each tree. Slide the little washi tape trees onto the string and enjoy. If you'd like the trees to stay evenly spaced on the string you can add a tiny glue dot to stop them from sliding around.

You now have a festive decoration! The options for these little trees are endless, as they would look darling as cupcake toppers or they would make fun gift tags.

FRAME ACCORDINGLY

This simple accordion tree is a combination of modern and rustic; the tree is on the modern side, while the frame calms this down with a more rustic feel. My favorite part is the washi tape background and how it appears to rise off the page, with a few pieces acting as a garland around the tree.

You will need:

- clear white lace washi tape
- yellow washi tape
- white card stock
- green card stock, shorter than the frame in length
- star craft punch or cutting die
- scoring board, such as the mini scoring board from Martha Stewart Crafts
- low temperature hot glue gun
- rectangle frame of any size
- piece of wood or a popsicle (lolly) stick
- small star ornament (optional)

1 Begin by covering the frame insert with neat rows of clear white lace washi tape, or any festive washi tape of your choice. The most important thing with this step is to make sure you line up the tape pieces well, so the patterns match as best as they can. Then secure the washi tape frame insert into the frame.

2 Using the scoring board, create evenly spaced score lines 1cm (½in) apart along the front of the green card stock. Once you have all the lines scored, fold the card stock in an accordion style (back and forth) (A) then press the folds firmly down to create clean, neat fold lines (B).

3 Using your low temperature hot glue gun, glue one end of the tree folds together so that your tree opens out like a fan: fixed tightly at the top end while wide at the bottom. Now attach the accordion tree to the frame insert: center the tree within the frame then glue it, pressing it down as it dries to secure it into place.

4 You can either make your own star, or use a small star ornament instead, as shown (B). To make the star, tape a few short rows of yellow tape onto the white card stock then use a star craft punch to punch it out.

5 Use the scoring board to give the star a three-dimensional appearance. To do this, just flip it over and score lines on the back from the tips of the star towards the center then fold along each score line.

You could easily make this festive decoration with any inexpensive frame.

B

A

6 Add the star to the top of the tree with a dab of hot glue. Just a dab will do ya!

7 For the tree trunk, just use your low temperature hot glue gun to attach the popsicle (lolly) stick to the covered frame at the bottom of the tree.

8 Finish the frame by draping a few pieces of tape diagonally around the tree to look like a garland (C).

There you have it! A festive decoration that will look great sitting on your mantle or hanging on a wall.

☉PULENT
ORNAMENTS

When it comes to ornaments,
I say the lighter the better! All the
handmade ornaments featured
here are lightweight, and just the
inspiration you'll need to create a
tree filled with that handmade touch.
In fact, you'll love to hang these on
your Christmas tree year after year;
whether it's a special first year in a
new home, a baby's first Christmas,
or a gift to a loved one, these
ornaments will become Christmas
keepsakes for your family.

TEENY TINY TREES

I'm a big fan of bottlebrush trees, and used together with these little wooden spools they look like mini Christmas trees in stands. The trick with these ornaments is finding a washi tape you love that's the same width as the little spools you are using.

You will need:

- washi tape in assorted festive designs
- glittery gold card stock
- star craft punch
- red and white baker's twine
- glue dots
- low temperature hot glue gun
- natural wooden spools
- tiny bottlebrush trees

1 Gather together all your supplies. Then just by eyeballing it, try to find a washi tape that will be a good size match for the little spools you have chosen.

2 Wrap a 7.5cm (3in) length of washi tape around your first spool. Depending on the stickiness of the washi tape you are using, you might need to add a little glue dot at the end to ensure the tape stays adhered to the spool.

3 Now use your low temperature hot glue gun to add a little glue to the end of a bottlebrush tree then insert the tree into the top hole of the spool. You can add more glue around the top rim of the spool to keep the tree centered.

4 Add a dab of glue to the top of the bottlebrush tree then attach a little looped and knotted piece of baker's twine to hang your tree from.

5 To finish off this little ornament, use the star craft punch to punch out a gold star from the glittery gold card stock then stick this over the glue to hide it.

Now you can hang this little ornament on your Christmas tree. It would make an adorable ornament for a baby's first Christmas: you could write the baby's name and the year on the bottom side of the spool to create a special keepsake. As with all the ornaments in this section, use little wire ornament hangers to make it easy to hang your creations on the tree.

You will need:

- washi tape in assorted festive designs
- heavy card stock or kraft paper
- 5cm (2in) round photos
- 8.75cm (3½in) scalloped circle craft punch or a regular circle craft punch
- die cutting tool, such as the CuttleBug from Cricut, or a craft knife
- 5cm (2in) circle cutting die
- red and white baker's twine
- glue dots
- heavy-duty needle
- paper punch and eyelet setter, such as Crop-A-Dile, with metal eyelets (all optional)

FRAME YOUR FAVORITE FACES

Photo ornaments are always treasured decorations on the Christmas tree. They capture who we are at a special moment in time then we get to pull them out every year and hang them on the tree at Christmas. These handmade washi tape photo ornaments are light in weight, but full of color and creativity. You can layer different patterns of washi tape to make bright, happy frames to fill with your favorite faces.

1 Start by covering the heavy card stock or kraft paper with 10cm (4in) lengths of washi tape. You can alternate between different tape designs, or you could apply one design leaving a blank space in between each strip. Have fun with this step and become creative.

2 Once you have your patterns in place, use the circle craft punch to punch out the circle shapes from each piece of card stock (A). I happened to be using a 8.75cm (3½in) scalloped circle punch, but you could use something smaller or larger with either a regular circle or a fancy edge.

3 Using the die cutting tool and the 5cm (2in) circle cutting die, now cut out a smaller center circle from each piece of the card stock to create the frames. If you don't have a die cutting tool, use a craft knife to do this instead: trace a smaller circle on the underside of the larger circle then cut out the center on a cutting mat.

4 With the larger circle craft punch, cut out more circles from the card stock to act as backs for the ornaments.

Instead of a needle, you could use a paper punch and eyelet setter to make a sturdier hole at the top of each frame to thread the baker's twine through.

A

B

5 Cut out the photos to fit the frames. You can cut them to fit underneath the covered circle frame, or you can cut them even smaller to show the exposed edge of the circle shaped photos (B).

6 Using glue dots, adhere the three circles of each frame grouping together: the photos, as well as the fronts and backs of the frames.

7 So these ornaments can hang from a Christmas tree, add long pieces of red and white baker's twine. Poke holes through the tops of the photo frames with a heavy-duty needle and thread twine through then tie a knot at the top (C).

Now for the fun part! Give these handmade ornaments as a gift, or keep them for yourself so you can enjoy them year after year on your tree.

C

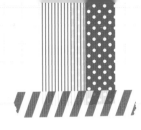

You will need:

- washi tape in assorted festive colors and designs
- 30 x 30cm (12 x 12in) white card stock
- circle craft punch, or die cutting tool and circle cutting dies, in one or two sizes
- red and white baker's twine
- low temperature hot glue gun
- small scoring board, such as the mini scoring board from Martha Stewart Crafts (optional)

JOLLY HOLIDAY BAUBLES

These beautiful baubles are great for hanging on both large and small Christmas trees because you can make them any size you want. They add a fun three-dimensional effect without being too heavy for the branches. They might look complex to make but they truly are easy, so gather together some friends for a fun night of Christmas crafting!

1 To start, tape a few rows of one washi tape design across one edge of the white card stock, lining up the patterns to match nicely. Then repeat this process with four different, yet coordinating, washi tape designs. By doing this along the edges of the card stock it will be easier to use a craft punch to cut them out.

2 Use your circle craft punch or die cutting tool to punch out a row of circles along the strips of washi tape.

3 To assemble one bauble, gather together five paper circles, each with a different washi tape pattern or all the same (be creative!). Fold each of the five circles in half, making a tight, neat crease down the center of each. You can use the scoring board if you'd like help with this.

4 With your glue gun warmed up and ready to go, cover one half of a paper circle with glue then adhere it to one half of another circle. Repeat this process until you reach the last two sides to glue together.

5 Depending on the size of the paper bauble you are making, you'll need a piece of baker's twine for the ornament to hang from. For the larger ones, I used a 15cm (6in) piece of baker's twine, and for the smaller ones, a 10cm (4in) piece. Fold the twine in half and tie a knot with the two ends together.

6 Before you hot glue the last two sides together, apply an extra dab of glue in the center and add the baker's twine. Press and hold as the hot glue sets to secure the last two sides together, and the twine in place.

There you go! Now you have a colorful lightweight adorable little ornament. You could also use these baubles as gift toppers or string a bunch together in a row on baker's twine as a garland.

SWEET CANDYLAND

Peppermint candies with their classic red and white swirls will always remind me of Christmas and of decorating gingerbread houses. This candy-like garland is a fun way to bring a 'Candyland' feel to your festivities and to guarantee sweet dreams ahead.

You will need:

- red and white washi tape in assorted designs
- pinking shears
- twine or string
- large wooden or plastic beads with a large (1cm/½in diameter) opening
- low temperature hot glue gun (optional)

1 To start, slide the beads onto the string or twine. If your beads are loose and sliding along the twine, you might want to secure them in place. Use your low temperature hot glue gun to apply evenly spaced dabs of hot glue along the twine then quickly slide the beads over the hot glue to secure.

2 Place a 7.5 to 10cm (3 to 4in) piece of washi tape on the table, sticky side up, and place a bead on top in the center. Now place a second piece of washi tape directly on top of the bottom piece, ensuring the patterns match for a smooth finish. However, it doesn't matter if the torn ends don't match in length, as you'll be trimming them.

3 Trim the ends with pinking shears to create a fancy, candy-like wrapper edge then just twist each end to make the covered bead look like a piece of candy.

Now you have a sweet-as-candy garland to add to your tree or your mantle; alternatively these candies would look cute on a wreath, too.

Not all of the washi tapes I used for this project completely covered each bead, which I'm okay with because the garland will generally be seen from afar. But if you'd like each bead to be completely covered, just double up the pieces of washi tape to make the coverage complete.

BEAUTIFUL BALLS AND STARS

You will need:

- gold striped washi tape, or design of your choice
- kraft card stock or paper
- paper slicer (guillotine)
- small paper punch
- twine or string
- small brass or silver brads

These beautiful paper ornaments are light and airy, and perfect for letting the twinkly lights on your tree shine through them. The ornaments can be anything you'd like them to be, depending on the pattern of washi tape you use and the style you choose to go with. Here I've provided four variations of the same ornament, some using two brads and some using only one.

1 Begin by adding long strips of washi tape to the kraft card stock. You could use any color of card stock for these ornaments, but I just really liked how the kraft paper looked covered with the gold striped washi tape.

2 Using your paper slicer (guillotine), slice along the edge of the washi tape to create neat strips measuring the same length and width. The strips here measured about 18cm (7in) in length, and about 1cm (½in) in width.

As you can see in the illustration, there are a few variations of this ornament and it's up to you how you'd like yours to look:

Ball

Line up six strips of washi tape then punch a hole through both ends of each strip. Using two brads, poke one of the brads through one end of all the pieces and secure together. Now fan out all the strips to create a circle. Using the second brad, add each strip onto this brad in its fanned-out state to create a globe-like ball then bend the brad back on itself to hold the pieces in place (A). Finish the ornament off by adding a little string or twine to the top brad so you can hang your ball from the tree.

It's up to you whether you choose to make these ornaments in the same shape using a variety of different washi tape patterns, or in different shapes using the same design, as you see here.

A

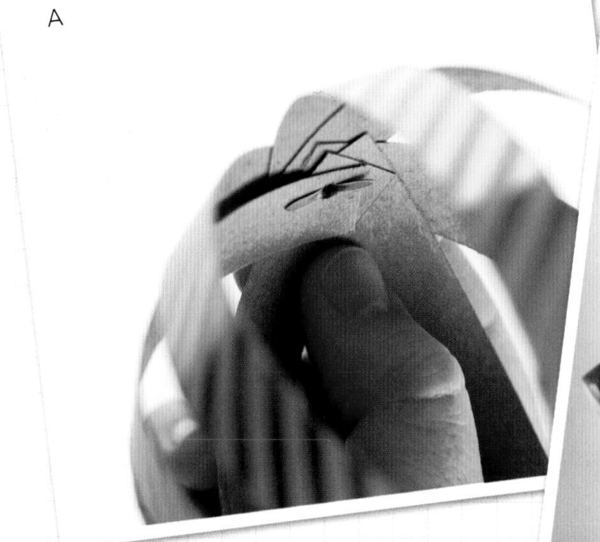

B

Star 1

Just like for the ball, follow all the same steps using two brads. However, once you have created the ball shape, smash this flat to create a crease on each strip to make it look more like a star. You could also make a crease on the strips before you add them to the brads to ensure they are evenly creased.

Star 2

Just like in Star 1, smash the strips of washi tape flat. But rather than using two brads, use just one and slide all the ends onto this (B).

Bubble loop

As in Star 2, use just one brad for this version. However, instead of creasing your strips, slightly bend each one so that both ends are on the same brad to create a pretty bubble loop look.

Get creative and have fun with these beautiful ornaments. Either way you choose to make them, they will look wonderful on your tree.

TABLE
TREASURES

There's no better way to spend
quality time with the ones you love
than by sharing a meal together, as
this is where memories are made.
Set the stage for a special night by
adding little handmade details to
your beautifully set table. Amongst
these projects you'll find terrific
table runners, pretty place settings,
cute cupcake toppers, and sweet
centerpieces to make your table shine.

TWINKLING TEA LIGHTS

The combination of inexpensive tea light candles and washi tape is a match made in heaven. Lots of twinkling lights really set the mood for a special dinner, so set the table with plenty of these little candles and enjoy the ambiance they bring to your gathering.

You will need:

- washi tape in assorted designs
- tea light candles
- matches
- baker's twine (optional)
- cellophane bags (optional)

1 Measure out lengths of washi tape that match the width of your candles. Then simply adhere these washi tape lengths carefully around the edges of the tea lights.

2 You might like to wrap a bundle of matches together with baker's twine to enhance your display. You can also package up a bunch of these cute candles in a cellophane bag as a gift for a neighbor or as a party favor; just don't forget to include the matches!

Arrange the candles on your table, light them and enjoy. Sometimes it's those simple details that make gatherings special.

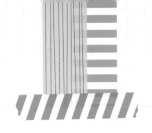

ALL ABOUT THE STRIPES

This simple idea for a table runner can make a strong statement on a beautifully set table. Sometimes it's the most simple ideas that can make the biggest impact.

You will need:

- same colored washi tape in assorted designs
- roll of white butcher paper (kraft paper)

1 Roll out a large piece of white butcher paper, depending on how you want your runner to fit your table: you can run the butcher paper all the way along the length of your table, or you can run it in small sections to hang across the table width.

2 Tear varying lengths of washi tape then adhere them across the center of the

butcher paper, leaving about 1 to 2.5cm (½ to 1in) of white space between each piece. I love the look of the torn edges of washi tape, but if you'd like clean straight edges, use scissors to cut your washi tape lengths instead.

So simple, yet a fantastic way to introduce color and impact to your table setting.

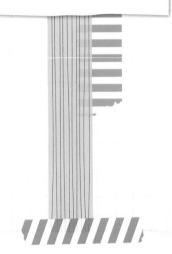

NATURAL PLACE SETTING

Make beautiful place settings for a special Christmas dinner using natural elements and washi tape.

You will need:

- washi tape
- garden trimmers
- small snips taken from your Christmas tree or a pine tree
- fine point permanent marker (optional)

1 Using garden trimmers, cut small little sprigs from either your real Christmas tree, a pine tree, or a bush outside. Sprigs of rosemary would work equally well for this project, too.

2 Using a little strip of washi tape in the color and design of your choice, just tape a little pine sprig down onto each plate. You could also write your guest's name on the tape to really personalize the place setting.

This is a simple way to bring elements of nature indoors and a nice way to celebrate the season.

You will need:

- similar colored washi tape in assorted designs
- white card stock
- small circle craft punch
- glue dots
- low temperature hot glue gun
- papier-mâché cones in two different sizes

CONFETTI CONE TREES

For a festive holiday centerpiece using all your favorite washi tapes, try these confetti cone trees. They're easy to make, plus they're confetti without all the mess!

1 Start by taping rows of washi tape in various designs along the edge of the white card stock, so the craft punch will cover the designs when you punch out the circles. Then punch out a bunch of little confetti circles, enough to cover all the cone trees you will be making.

2 Starting at the bottom and working around each tree in a circle, use glue dots to adhere each little piece of confetti to the cones, layering these circles so they are just slightly overlapping each other. As you complete each row, move up to the next and continue the pattern until you reach the top of your tree.

3 Using your low temperature hot glue gun, glue down any pieces that aren't sticking very well or looking as you'd like them to. If you have extra confetti circles when you're finished, use them to decorate the table around the trees.

Now you have a few cute Christmas centerpieces for a special dinner or dessert table.

STUNNING SNOW GLOBES

Sometimes finding a new use for your craft supplies can be so much fun! Try using your favorite washi tapes as ornament holders to keep glass or plastic ball ornaments from rolling around on your table displays. Rolls of washi tape are ideal for holding them upright, and they work really well as part of a pretty place setting.

You will need:

- washi tape rolls
- baker's twine
- snow-like glitter
- tiny green bottlebrush trees
- old–fashioned lightbulb–shaped ornaments in glass or plastic

1 Make a little snow globe by inserting a tiny bottlebrush tree into a glass or plastic ornament then add snow-like glitter to create the appearance of a wintery tree scene. Finish your snow globe by tying some red and white baker's twine in a bow to the top.

2 Place your ornament inside a roll of washi tape at your place setting to keep it upright and in place.

This is such a simple yet darling way to welcome guests to a special dinner. You can even send them home with the ornament and washi tape as a party favor for a fun way to remember the night.

Instead of creating your own old–fashioned Christmas lightbulb ornaments specially, you could always just use your own glass or plastic ball ornaments.

NOEL, NOEL

Spell out the beautiful word 'Noel' with patterns of washi tape then use this to top a cake or a batch of cupcakes – you could use it as a banner, as well.

You will need:

- washi tape in assorted designs
- Noel template (see Templates)
- fine-tip scissors
- clear sticky tape
- wooden skewers

1 Make a photocopy of the Noel template then start taping rows of washi tape over each of the block letters so you completely cover them.

2 Using your fine-tip scissors, carefully cut out each letter then use clear sticky tape on their backs to adhere them onto wooden skewers.

Now you can insert your letters into cupcakes, or add them to the top of a beautiful cake, as a fun way to wish friends and family a very Merry Christmas.

If you'd like to make these letters into a garland instead, just grab some twine (red and white baker's twine would be cute) or string. Space the letters out how you'd like them on the string then use either natural clothes pins (pegs) to hang them, or adhere your letters with glue dots for a more permanent display.

GORGEOUS GIFTS

You just can't beat a handmade gift: the attention to detail, knowing that it was made with someone special in mind, and that it came from the heart are all reasons to celebrate and enjoy it. Here you'll find ideas that will inspire you to add handmade touches to gifts that the recipients can enjoy early during the Christmas season and throughout the rest of the year.

You will need:

- washi tape in assorted designs
- kraft paper card set (cards and envelopes)
- 30 x 30cm (12 x 12in) pieces of white card stock
- circle craft punch
- scoring board
- pencils
- journal
- baker's twine
- paper clips
- lace paper doily
- gift tag
- gift container

SPLENDID STATIONERY

Everyone loves stationery, so get crafty and create your own stationery gift sets, personalized with gorgeous washi tape designs. Sending off a quick thank you note will become an easy and enjoyable task for the lucky recipients of this fun little set.

1 Start by wrapping a few new pencils with washi tape in different designs then decorate a new journal with washi tape to coordinate your gift set together.

2 Transform paper clips into bookmark flags by folding short pieces of washi tape around their ends then trimming these to make them look finished.

3 Wrap the cards together with a paper doily and a white card stock circle, cut out from a circle craft punch and decorated with washi tape. Then tie them all together using a piece of baker's twine.

4 To make envelope liners, cover the corners of the 30 x 30cm (12 x 12in) white card stock with washi tape then trim to fit into the envelopes – these don't need to

be measured perfectly. Use the scoring board to make a neat crease so that each liner will fold with its envelope then use a few glue dots to secure it in place.

5 To finish, package all your items together in a suitable container to create your gift set. A simple gift tag is a great place to hold all the paper clips in one spot, and you can decorate the gift tag with matching washi tape for a fun look.

Someone lucky would be thrilled to receive this pretty stationery set as a gift that they can use all year long.

BRILLIANT BAKING

The Christmas season is a wonderful time to get baking in the kitchen. So why not create a special baking gift set filled with washi tape flags to top cakes and cupcakes? Be sure to also include decorative cupcake liners and a few other odds and ends to complete this sweet little baking set.

You will need:

- washi tape in assorted holiday colors and designs
- fine-tip scissors
- baker's twine
- red ribbon for a bow
- cupcake liners
- sprinkles and colored sugars
- white paper lollipop sticks
- wooden spoon
- cupcake baking pan
- cake mix (optional)

1 Begin by creating some little washi tape flags as cupcake toppers. To make one, pull out a length of washi tape, position a white paper lollipop stick onto it then wrap the tape around it, leaving a section hanging out like a flag. Give the flag a decorative edge by using a pair of fine-tip scissors to notch the ends into a V shape.

2 Continue to make more flags in the way described in step 1 then tie all the flags together with a little bow of baker's twine. Also wrap the wooden spoon with some strips of washi tape in different designs for a festive decorative look.

3 Gather together all your supplies for the kit, including a few different cupcake liners (A). Using the cupcake baking tin as your container, fill it with the liners, flags, and sprinkles. Then wrap this all up with a big bow to finish it off.

Now you have an adorable gift that any baker would love to receive – young, old, seasoned or novice. Let the baking season begin!

Not all washi tape has the same stickiness, so you might need to add a little glue dot to secure the washi tape onto the wooden spoon.

A

THAT'S A WRAP

Give the gift to create beautifully wrapped presents with this crafty giftwrap set. Check your list off early by handing out this set at the very beginning of the holiday season. Your friends and family will love being given so many options for wrapping presents.

You will need:

- washi tape in assorted festive colors and designs
- old fashioned natural clothes pins (pegs)
- candy cane striped pipe cleaners
- gift tags
- stickers
- ribbon
- buttons
- jingle bells
- pom-poms
- other mini gift toppers of your choice
- festive container

1 Wrap long lengths of washi tape measuring about 30 to 36cm (1 to 2ft) around your old fashioned wooden clothes pins (pegs) (A). Depending on the width of the washi tape, you should be able to fit three or four different patterns around each clothes pin.

2 Now gather up your favorite fancy gift toppers including gift tags, stickers, jingle bells, pom-poms, ribbons, and candy cane striped pipe cleaners for more three-dimensional gift tags and toppers, and add anything more you'd like to include in your gift set.

3 To share your fun washi tape collection, arrange these items in a festive container along with your decorative clothes pins. And that's it!

Let your friends enjoy all the new options they now have for decorating and topping presents during this wonderful gift-giving season.

A

CHOCOLATE CELEBRATION

Everyone loves a sweet treat, and if it includes chocolate, even better! Add a little decorative wrap to mini chocolate bars then fill a mason jar with these cute candies as a gift for a neighbor or a great teacher.

You will need:

- washi tape in assorted colors and designs
- 30 x 30cm (12 x 12in) white card stock
- paper slicer (guillotine)
- baker's twine
- glue dots
- bag of miniature chocolate bars with gold and silver wrappers
- mason jar

1 Using the paper slicer (guillotine), cut the white card stock into strips measuring 2.5cm (1in) wide by 7.5cm (3in) long.

2 Tape pieces of washi tape with different designs onto the white paper strips then wrap a strip around each little candy bar (A). Secure them in place with a glue dot.

3 Fill a mason jar with these cute chocolates and tie a bow of baker's twine around the neck of the jar. You can add a gift card too, if you'd like.

This gift of chocolate with a crafty touch is sure to make someone very happy.

A CHARMING GIFT

A beautiful necklace personalized for someone special makes such a thoughtful gift. These necklaces are all made using different patterns of washi tape: you'll be using washi tape to create a background for the tiny necklace charms, and you'll also use washi tape to make coordinating packaging for the necklaces to be wrapped up in.

You will need:

- washi tape
- white card stock
- fine-tip scissors
- decorative edge scissors, or die cutting tool and cutting die
- low temperature hot glue gun
- blank metal charms
- long necklace chains
- tiny charms and flower embellishments
- natural brown gift boxes

1 Begin by taping a few rows of your favorite washi tape designs together onto white card stock to create a pattern to fill the back of a blank metal charm. Lay the blank charm on top of the washi taped card stock and trace around it, then cut out the shape so that it fits snuggly into the charm (A).

2 Using your low temperature hot glue gun, add a dab of glue to the center of the metal charm to secure the washi tape design into it. Add another dab of glue at the top center of the charm to fix in place your tiny charm or flower.

3 Now attach your charm to a nice long chain so it's easy to wear, as well as easy to put on and take off.

4 For a fun way to package your necklace, make a matching background to display your handmade charm. Simply tape rows of washi tape to white card stock, then trim using decorative scissors or a die cutting tool to fit into the gift box. Layer a piece of plain white card stock with the same fancy scalloped edge behind it to make the colors pop!

This handmade charm works great as a necklace, but would be darling as a key chain as well.

Cut a little notch in the center of the packaging to slide the chain down so the charm lays centered in the gift box.

A

WONDROUS WRAPPING

The wrap job on a gift is where it's at!
Paying attention to these details can
really let your friends and family know
you took extra care in making their
gift special. So this is your chance to
showcase your creativity and launch
yourself into the giving season.
Whoever is lucky on your list this year
will be wowed! Here are a few ideas
to inspire you to add a handmade
detail here and there to make your
gift wrapping really stand out as
something great.

LOVELY LOLLIPOPS

You will need:

- rainbow assortment of washi tape
- 30 x 30cm (12 x 12in) white card stock
- 4cm (1½in) circle craft punch or cutting die
- glue dots with a strong adhesive
- 2.5cm (1in) diameter clear plastic tubes that fit larger gumballs
- sturdy piece of chipboard for the base

The classic line from the book *The Night Before Christmas* reads 'The children were nestled all snug in their beds, while visions of sugar-plums danced in their heads', and the inspiration for this sweet treat all started with that well known line. A clear tube filled with a rainbow of gumballs is finished off with a lollipop top made from washi tape. Gather up all your favorite washi tapes in a rainbow of colors and patterns to make this wonderfully fun gift topper.

1 Line up your washi tapes in rainbow order and begin taping a couple of rows of each color to the white card stock. If you're using a circle paper punch, make sure that the patterns you use will fill the circle once punched out. Also, depending on the width of the washi tapes you use, you might need to line up more than two rows of the same pattern to punch out each circle.

2 Punch out all your circles then use them to create the washi tape lollipop. Starting with one color of the rainbow, add a little glue dot to one side of the circle then stick it onto the next color circle in line. Continue adding adhesive to the bottom of each circle as you work your way around to make your paper lollipop. You'll find that while the glue dots are a secure adhesive, they also have a little give, making it possible to move the circles around as needed.

3 Finish off your big washi tape lollipop by adding a sturdy piece of chipboard to the back of it, securing this in place with a few more glue dots. Now for the fun part: fill a clear plastic tube with a rainbow assortment of gumballs then just tape the lollipop to the top.

This makes for a sweet and colorful treat that anyone would love, both kids and adults alike.

BAGGED WITH A BOW

Whether giving a homemade treat or store-bought candy, this handmade washi tape bow is a darling way to wrap it up. The nice thing about this bow is that when it's attached to a clothes pin (peg), you can sneak a treat out of the bag during the day then easily close the treat bag back up! I've filled these little bags with mini candy canes, cinnamon hearts and chocolate covered cinnamon bears, my favorite treat! (It's a Utah thing.)

You will need

- washi tape in assorted festive colors and designs
- paper doilies
- fine-tip scissors
- heavy-duty glue dots
- 30cm (12in) ruler
- standard sized clothes pins (pegs)
- clear cellophane bags
- candy or homemade treat

1 Start by using the ruler to cut three different lengths of washi tape for the bow: large (40.5cm/16in), medium (20cm/8in) and small (2.5cm/1in). The long strip will create the main piece of the bow looping in on itself, the medium piece will form the back of the bow with the ends notched out, and the short piece will be wrapped around both holding them together.

2 Fold the long piece of washi tape in half and tape it to itself, creating a 20cm (8in) piece of washi tape with no sticky sides exposed.

3 Repeat step 2 with the medium length piece, so that you end up with a 10cm (4in) piece of washi tape, with no sticky sides exposed.

4 Take the longer of these two pieces and fold it in half again. With fine-tip scissors, notch out the edge of each side to create a more narrow section at both the folded end and the other end of the piece (A).

5 Repeat step 4 using the medium length piece, only this time use your scissors to notch out an upside down V shape on the ends, as these will be the decorative ends of the bow.

6 Open out and place a heavy-duty glue dot in the center of the fold of the long piece (B). Now take both narrow ends and adhere them to the glue dot then press firmly to secure the ends, thus creating the two loops of the bow on your longest piece (C).

7 Open out the medium length piece then use a second glue dot to adhere the large looped piece to the center of the medium one.

Instead of using heavy-duty glue dots, you could use a low temperature hot glue gun for this project.

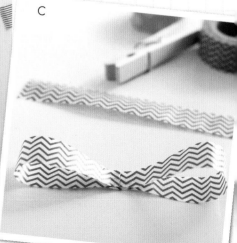

8 Fold your smallest strip in on itself lengthways to create a narrower piece then use a third glue dot to tightly adhere it around the bow.

9 With a final heavy-duty glue dot, adhere the washi tape bow to the center of your clothes pin (peg).

10 To assemble your goodie bag, just fill the clear cellophane bag with candy or treats, fold over the top, then fold the paper doily in half over the top and finish it off with your handmade washi tape bow clothes pin (D).

This is an edible handmade treat that your neighbors, family and friends will love to receive.

D

SNEAK-A-PEEK PACKS

Allow your homemade treat to peek through these cute little packages. The small handmade wreath you'll make to sit around the clear window of the packaging is a festive nod to Christmas.

You will need:

- washi tape in assorted colors
- 30 x 30cm (12 x 12in) white card stock
- kraft boxes with or without clear plastic windows (if without, boxes should be small enough to run through your die cutting tool)
- 1.25cm (½in) circle craft punch
- red twine or string
- glue dots
- die cutting tool with 5cm (2in) circle cutting die (optional)

1 To create boxes with a peek-through window, run each box flat through a die cutting tool, cutting through just one side. To cut through only one layer of the box, the cutting die needs to rest in between the two layers of the flat gift box. When you assemble the box afterwards, tape a piece of clear plastic cellophane on the inside to create a peek-through window pane.

2 To create the circle wreath on your box, tape a piece of washi tape to the edge of the white card stock. Then use your small circle craft punch to create a bunch of tiny round cut-outs.

3 Adhere these little circle cut-outs around the peek-through window using glue dots. Finish the little wreath off by using a glue dot to attach a little red twine tied in a bow.

If you whipped up something sweet to give as a gift, these little peek-through packages will be the perfect container to show off your homemade treat.

MERRY MITTENS

Send warm wishes to the ones you love with these darling handmade mitten tags. There's something sweet about mittens, and maybe it's that most adults seem to grow out of them and move onto boring old gloves (womp-womp). But mittens seem to remind us of those old fashioned sleigh ride songs we all love to sing about this time of year: 'Dashing through the snow…'

You will need:

- washi tape in your favorite holiday colors and designs
- Mittens template (see Templates)
- paper punch
- fine-tip scissors
- red twine

1 To start, make a photocopy of the mittens template onto card stock then begin taping rows of your favorite holiday washi tape designs directly over the mitten outlines.

2 Cut out each individual mitten then punch a tiny hole in the top corners of a mitten pair.

3 String a little red twine through the hole to attach the mittens together and tie a bow. Stick the bow to your present for a darling gift tag.

You can sign your name and write festive greetings on the reverse side of your mittens with warm wishes.

PLAYFUL PINWHEELS

You will need:

- washi tape
- white paper cut into squares to fit the top of your gift boxes
- long reach paper punch
- fine-tip scissors
- brads
- clear sticky tape

Typically a pinwheel is something that reminds us of springtime, but it's such a classic shape that it really needs to be used all year round. Plus its design makes the perfect gift topper to show off your favorite washi tape patterns.

1 To make one pinwheel, start attaching rows of washi tape to both sides of a white paper square. You could use card stock here, but I think a thinner piece of paper works better.

2 Once you have a washi tape pattern on both sides of your square, trim off the torn edges to create a clean square. Then use a long reach paper punch to punch a tiny hole in the center of the square.

3 Using fine-tip scissors , cut diagonal lines from each corner of the square to almost mid center, but take care not to cut all the way to the center. Then punch tiny holes in the right corner of each side (A).

4 Now you're ready to bend the square into a pinwheel shape. Grab a small brad and poke it through the hole on each corner around the square in turn (B).

5 Finish off by inserting the same brad through the center hole. Bend the ends of the brad to hold all the corners of the paper together in the center (C).

6 Add this cute gift topper to any box with a little piece of clear sticky tape.

There you have it, a happy way to finish off your Christmas gifts this year! These pinwheel gift toppers would also look darling all lined up as party favors, or snuck into a stocking.

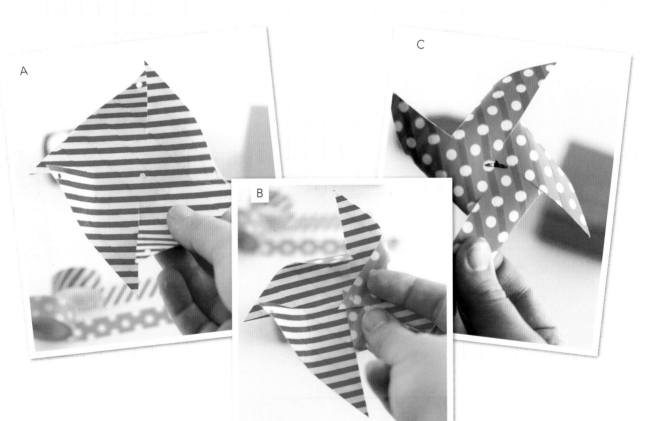

A

B

C

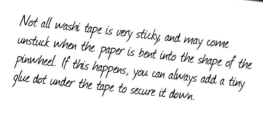

Not all washi tape is very sticky, and may come unstuck when the paper is bent into the shape of the pinwheel. If this happens, you can always add a tiny glue dot under the tape to secure it down.

TEMPLATES

The templates used in the projects are provided here at actual size. To use, simply photocopy or scan then print the book page and use as described in the corresponding project. Alternatively, you can download a printable PDF of the templates from the following website: www.stitchcraftcreate.co.uk/patterns

HOLLY BERRY

NOEL

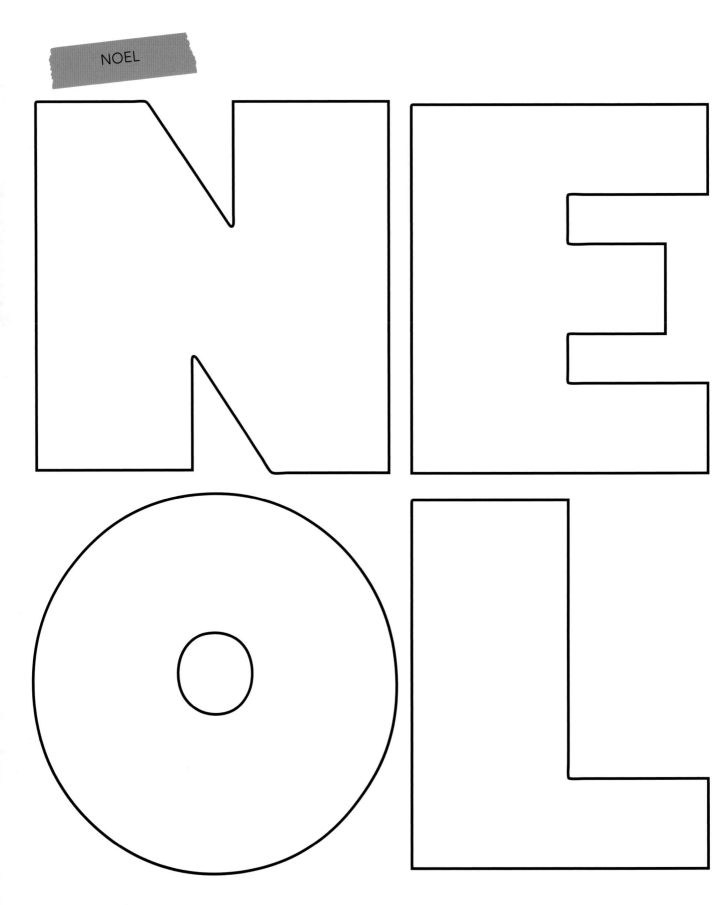

ABOUT THE AUTHOR

Kami Bigler lives in Utah with her family. She began blogging in 2007, and you can still find her sharing creative ideas every week at NoBiggie (www.nobiggie.net), a site filled with fun holiday ideas, recipes, free printables and lots more. Her obsession with washi tape started early and she's now lost count of how many rolls fill her craft desk. Kami's biggest accomplishment is being a wife and a mother to her darling kids. She loves to fill her days with blogging, cooking, crafting, thrifting, 'washi-ing' (it's a new word!) and a dirty Diet Pepsi... all the good stuff!

ACKNOWLEDGMENTS

Big thank yous:

To my biggest support and No 1 fan, my wonderful husband Kyle who has never stopped giving me encouragement and support as I make my creative dreams come true. To my cutest kids (Avery, Aiden, Afton…and Rukkus) for being my ultimate creative inspiration. To my wonderful friends and family who have been such a positive influence in my life. To my kind blog readers who swing by NoBiggie daily and leave the kindest comments even on days when it's a craft fail. To the team at FW Media for believing in me to make this book come to life. And to my ultimate example, our savior Jesus Christ, the reason for this wonderful Christmas season.

Wishing the Merriest Christmas to you and yours,

xoxo Kami